THE CIGAR INDUSTRY

You may have noticed that one of Cuba's biggest crops is tobacco. Most often, this tobacco is made into cigars. Then these cigars are sold to the rest of the world.

Cuban cigars are considered by many smokers to be the finest cigars available. This is partly due to the fact that Cuban cigars are made entirely by hand. Even Fidel Castro enjoyed Cuban cigars until he gave up smoking in 1985.

However, as long as the **embargo** with Cuba remains in effect, Cuban cigars are considered illegal in the United States.

A Cuban man rolls cigars.

GLOSSARY

allied (AL EYED) — friendly with

ancestry (AN SES tree) — a person's family history

banned (BAND) — not allowed

complex (KOM PLEKS) — complicated

embargo (em BAR go) — trade restriction

emigrate (EM uh GRAYT) — to leave a country to live somewhere else

fertile (FURT il) — good for growing

liberation (LIB ur ay shun) — to set free

literacy (LIT uh ruh see) — the ability to read and write

negotiation (neh GO shee ay shun) — communicating; working with

nuclear (NOO klee uhr) — using the power of the atom

FURTHER READING

Find out more about Cuba with these helpful books:

- Bramwell, Martyn. *The World in Maps: North America and the Caribbean.* Lerner Publications, 2000.
- Fox, Mary Virginia. *Modern World Nations: Cuba*. Lucent Books, 1999.
- Frank, Nicole, and Mark Cramer. *Countries of the World: Cuba*. Gareth Stevens, 2000.
- Frost, Helen. *A Look at Cuba (Our World)*. Pebble Books, 2002
- Hernandez, Roger E., and James D. Henderson. *Cuba*. Mason Crest Publishers, 2003.
- Morrison, Marion. *Enchantment of the World: Cuba*. Children's Press, 1999.

WEBSITES TO VISIT

- www.infoplease.com/ce6/world/A0814195.html
  Infoplease – Cuba
- www.infoplease.com/ce6/people/A0810800.html
  Infoplease – Fidel Castro

INDEX

About the Author

Kieran Walsh is a writer of children's nonfiction books, primarily on historical and social studies topics. Walsh has been involved in the children's book field as editor, proofreader, and illustrator as well as author.